Shakespeare and Germany
– Primary Source Edition

Henry Arthur Jones

SHAKESPEARE AND GERMANY

HE German newspapers are making merry over the prospect of our forthcoming national celebration of Shakespeare's Tercentenary. The "Times" of March 31d quotes the "Cologne Gazette" as follows

All Germany will contemplate this celebration with amused expectation and the utmost satisfaction. The English could give us no greater pleasure. The music hall and cinematograph spirit of the England of to-day will make such a mess of it that unquenchable laughter will run through the whole of Europe. The Quadruple Entente Shakespeare will be fêted with Maori dances, Japanese acrobats' tricks, and Tarantella leaps. To complete the festival only one thing is lacking—that the dead Shakespeare should express his opinion of the living England

From other German sources we learn that Shakespeare is essentially a German in his ideas and his conception of human affairs; that if he were alive he would be enthusiastically pro-German in his sympathies, that if England to-day were possessed with his spirit we should have won the war, that a true understanding and a worthy stage interpretation of Shakespeare are to be found only in Germany.

Taken altogether the recent German claims on Shakespeare are tokens of that same virulent epidemic of diseased brag which also claims for German prowess every valuable discovery in science, and all that is excellent in modern civilization.

With this constant evidence before us of German temper and methods, it will be well for England to be prepared for the characteristic official announcement which will doubtless be made in Berlin on 23rd April of the final and complete annexation by Germany of William Shakespeare, with all his literary, poetical, philosophical, and stage appurtenances, effects, traditions, and associations, and all the demesnes that there adjacent lie. Meantime we may ask by what insolence of egotism, what lust of plunder, or what madness of pride Germany dares add to the hideous roll of her thieveries and rapes this topping impudence and crime of vaunting to herself the allegiance of Shakespeare? Even were England as sunken and decrepit, as degraded and supine as Germany hugs herself to believe, yet Shakespeare, as he himself shall testify, would never abate the infinite measure of his love and loyalty for her whose jesses are his dear heartstrings

England may rest in great peace about Shakespeare's constancy to her. "They'll never depose me to make *you* King," said Charles II to James.

Every dramatist's work, so far as it has any value at all, of necessity reveals his attitude towards the permanent verities of human nature, and the great issues of life, and also towards the fashions and problems of his own day and his own society. This revelation of his general standpoint is often a fully self-conscious one But beyond this general, oblique, implicit, indication of his relation to the great mundane movement, every dramatist, however balanced and aloof he may strive to be, does also scatter through his work stray proofs of his own personal prejudices, opinions, and foibles, and also of the dominant passions and prepossessions of his soul. Sometimes this assertion of his own personal likes and dislikes and fixed ideas is also self-conscious and intentional

Why shouldn't it be? The dramatist is gagged and fettered by stricter and severer laws than any of his brother artists. No rule of his art forbids the novelist to air his own views, or to break out in purple patches on every page. And the actor often makes his greatest hit with the public when he deletes the author's words, obliterates his meaning and resplendently launches his own gag, or his own private emphasis, or when he bundles the author's character clean off the stage and substitutes his own popular personality

Why, then, shouldn't the dramatist—God help him otherwise, poor man!—occasionally take his private impulses and prepossessions for a swaggering parade on their own account? This is what Shakespeare often does Like Joe Gargery, he shuts up shop at any moment, and goes on his jaunts without any thought for the convenience of his customers, and though some necessary question of the play is then to be considered, he puts it aside, while he gives full tongue and strut to some glorious mouthing malapropos of his own

Of all the dominant prepossessions of Shakespeare's soul, those central fires and passions of his being that thus spontaneously leap out, and hint or betray the guarded secrets within his breast—fierce hatred of the mob, admiration for kingliness; admiration for chivalrous soldiership, contempt for priests and priestcraft, the dread apprehension of insomnia, the sense of the stupendous aimlessness and transcience of human life and effort as of vain shadows, inconsequent as a dream, empty and noisy and furious as an idiot's tale—of all these recurrent ideas and prepossessions, there is none more fundamental, more constantly operative, more magnificently emergent than his uncontrollable love for England as England As in Milton, it sometimes reaches to a prophetic strain. It has the unabashed pride and willing blindness of a lover's infatuation Much of Shakespeare's love for England is so native and assured, that it does not need to speak, but only glances and throbs It is always there, ready to burst out in unexpected places, and from unlikely persons, as when it suddenly transforms the dull fool Cloten into a sturdy, eloquent patriot Often it does not speak, but when it does speak——

Take away from Shakespeare all this native, intrinsic, allusive, unspoken love for England, and we will readily make a present of him to Germany along with those other renegades who made England's hour of trial and need the occasion to testify their hate of her, or to show off their mischievous, perverted cleverness, like a fool who cannot cease to play his accustomed pranks on the Day of Judgment. Germany delights to welcome and honour these renegades, we delight to kick them to her.

Start a poet on the theme of his country and we immediately take the measure of him. Shakespeare's love for England, always hotly smouldering through his plays, breaks out in many jets and spires that curl round her in little intromissary endearments and caresses —"Gracious England"; "England's blessed shore", "Dear Mother England," and a hundred others. While in "King John" and "Richard II" he flames up in great starry pointing pyramids of devotion and adoration for her.

It is scarcely likely that the Germans will act "King John" and "Richard II" at their Shakespearean Tercentenary Celebration. But if they wish to know what would be Shakespeare's feelings for England if he were alive to-day, let them carefully study the well-known passages in the first scenes of the second acts in each of these plays. They will then get their answer not from the lips of Shakespeare's characters, Austria and John of Gaunt, but from the veritable lips and inmost heart of Shakespeare himself.

In "King John" Austria is the enemy of England. A poorish creature, with a calfskin hanging round his own recreant limbs, he yet sells the lion's skin before he has killed him. He is assuring his ally that England shall be conquered and shall make submission

Austria [*Speaking to his ally.*]
  Upon thy cheek I lay this zealous kiss,
  As seal to this indenture of my love,

> That to my home I will no more return,
> Till Angiers and the right thou hast in France,
> Together with that pale, that white-faced shore,

Austria is going on to announce the imminent capture of England. This is too much for Shakespeare He shuts Austria's mouth, hustles him off the scene, and to the woeful confusion of dramatic propriety, continues Austria's speech in his own person, breaking out into rapturous adoration of England, proclaiming her impregnable and inviolable

> Whose foot spurns back the ocean's roaring tides,
> And coops from other lands her islanders,
> Even till that England, hedged in with the main,
> That water-walled bulwark, still secure
> And confident from foreign purposes,
> Even till that utmost corner of the west

Having thus discharged his own sentiments and convictions, Shakespeare retires and allows Austria to finish the speech, with a notable and fitting declension into bathos, or with a little hidden sting of irony, according as we may take it

> Even till that utmost corner of the west
> Salute thee for her King; till then, fair boy,
> Will I not think of home, but follow arms

Let Germans dissect and digest that speech before they boast that Shakespeare's sympathy and allegiance would have gone to them in this war.

Again, let Germans note and apply to the present situation the closing speech of King John, where the rich, deep diapason of Shakespeare's love for England again enlarges its compass, and ceases in a triumphant assurance to Germany that, unless England helps to wound itself, it shall never lie at the proud foot of a conqueror, and a triumphant assurance to England that the three corners of the world shall not shock her if she obeys the very simple condition of resting true to herself.

But if in "King John" Shakespeare sufficiently derides and tramples on these German boasts of his allegiance, what shall we say of "Richard II"? Let Germans undeaf their ears, and bring their acknowledged and unrivalled powers of critical analysis to the study of the ever quoted, never stale, dying speech of John of Gaunt

> *Gaunt* Methinks I am a prophet new inspired,
> And thus expiring do foretell of him
> His rash fierce blaze of riot cannot last,
> For violent fires soon burn out themselves,
> Small showers last long, but sudden storms are short,
> He tires betimes that spurs too fast betimes,
> With eager feeding food doth choke the feeder
> Light vanity, insatiate cormorant,
> Consuming means, soon preys upon itself

This is rather poor stuff. John of Gaunt gets tired of it, and finding it hopeless to prophesy about Richard II, begins to prophesy about England Shakespeare gets tired of it, and shuts it off. Suddenly, from this common-place level of jingling platitudes, his love for England blazes out, with no cause of ignition, and springs upward like a pyramid of fire.

> This royal throne of Kings, this sceptred isle,
> This earth of majesty, this seat of Mars,
> This other Eden, demi-paradise,
> This fortress built by Nature for herself
> Against infection and the hand of war,
> This happy breed of men, this little world,
> This precious stone set in the silver sea,
> Which serves it in the office of a wall,
> Or as a moat defensive to a house
> Against the envy of less happier lands,
> This blessed spot, this earth, this realm, this England,
> This nurse, this teeming womb of royal Kings,
> Feared by their breed, and famous by their birth,
> Renowned for their deeds as far from home,
> For Christian service and true chivalry,
> As is the sepulchre in stubborn Jewry
> Of the world's ransom, blessed Mary's son.

This land of such dear souls, this dear, dear land,
Dear for her reputation through the world,
Is now leased out (I die pronouncing it)
Like to a tenement, or pelting farm
England bound in with the triumphant sea,
Whose rocky shore beats back the envious siege
Of watery Neptune, is now bound in with shame,
With inky blots and rotten parchment bonds,
That England that was wont to conquer others
Hath made a shameful conquest of itself
Ah! would the scandal vanish with my life,
How happy then were my ensuing death!

Again the speech is an intromission. It is not connected with the preceding platitudes, and only by an evident transition does it fall into its appropriate dramatic conclusion. It is Shakespeare himself who is speaking, with what Coleridge would have called a superfoetation of his own love and patriotism. He has not treated John of Gaunt quite so unceremoniously as he treated Austria He has not pushed him off the scene and taken the entire stage to himself. Yet it is clear that throughout the great, spontaneous outburst Shakespeare himself is speaking through the thin and transparent mask of John of Gaunt. Surely it will need a more than German density of ingenious misapprehension and talent for laborious misconstruction, to interpret that passage as anything but a defiant foresight and resolution of Shakespeare to remain an Englishman, in spite of all temptation to belong to another nation And that nation Germany! And that Germany the Germany of Wilhelm and Von Tirpitz!

So bad begins and worse remains behind Only one thing is lacking to fill the measure of Germany's joy and triumph in their imaginary capture of Shakespeare— "that the dead Shakespeare should express his opinion of the living England"

Well, he has expressed it They shall have their answer from his own lips By what magic of prophetic

mockery does Shakespeare again forestall and flout
these German attempts to appropriate his loyalty with
the rest of their ill-gotten prey and plunder? For in this
very speech, Shakespeare, with his well accredited gift
of universal prevision, has abundantly given them satisfaction

Let German critics rub their spectacles, and purge
their eyes, and read the speech again The England of
that day is described in the text It was "bound in with
shame" It had "become a tenement or pelting (paltry)
farm." England that was wont to conquer others, had
" made a shameful conquest of itself." It was a manifest
" scandal" Indeed, the state of England then was very
much what the Germans suppose (alas! not without
some show of proof) to be the state of England to-day.
In that respect Shakespeare grants them all they ask

Yet this opprobrious moment, when England was
" bound in with shame," is the very moment that Shakespeare chooses to lavish upon her the utmost ecstasies
of his love and devotion; to stand upon the mountain-
top of poetry and there to trumpet the loud pride of his
patriotism for her in waves and waves and resurgent
waves of triumphant music, that still rolls on the universal air, the alarum to our responding pride of patriotism
for her to-day, from the northernmost tip of the Shetlands,
westward over the blossoming solitudes of Canada, to
the southernmost cape of New Zealand.

And he does this for a personal, not for a dramatic
reason—for no cause—except the necessary and obvious
one of confuting these latter-day German pretensions
to him

Shakespeare forsake England! Leave this blessed
plot, this dear, dear land, to become the laureate of
Louvain, to hang chaplets of song on the ruins of
Rheims; to pipe to the German dance of lust and arson
and blood; to chant pæans of victory over murdered
babes; to shower canticles of benediction over the pirates
that sunk the " Lusitania," the vultures that tore out the

entrails of Belgium, the bandits that have desolated
Europe! Let not the fond Germans imagine it! Let
them rather imagine anything that is most unimagin-
able,—Hindenburg marching into London, and Wilhelm
anointed in Westminster Abbey with the chrism of
English mothers' tears, the spatter of English children's
brains, and the smear of ravished English maidenhood
Let Germans fondly imagine that, but let them not imagine that if Shakespeare were alive to-day, his pen
would scratch one syllable till he had engraved on their
foreheads in characters redder and starker than the sign
on the forehead of Cain, the blazon of his uncontrollable
hate for the Germany of to-day; there to remain visible
and enduring till civilization has perished and time has
forgotten itself.

Some rashness and ingenuity of presumption are
needed to prescribe what Shakespeare would be doing
and saying if he were alive to-day Certain it is that he
would not be asking for a safe passage to Berlin, there
to take out his papers of naturalization. It has been sug-
gested that he might be usefully occupied in attending
the committee meetings of the Shakespeare Memorial
Theatre. And again that he would be busily engaged in
casting and rehearsing those of his plays that are pre-
sently to be performed, and cutting and adapting them
to modern English taste Those who are unable, without
a shock of incongruity, to picture Shakespeare as taking
anything more than a benevolently neutral interest in
these undertakings, may amuse themselves with the
pleasing thought that if he were alive to-day, he would
be congenially employed in hounding and routing all
the legion tribes of cranks, freaks, windbags, wordsters,
and impossibilists that infest our land; all the crazy
pacifists, whose mewlings and pukings have brought
about this war, all the slugabeds and time-servers and
pleasure-seekers, that have lulled themselves with the
sleepy drench of that lake of forgetfulness and sloth,
wherein England has lain sprawling for the last genera-

tion, all the nest of petty traitors who have proclaimed
their topsy-turvy patriotism for every country but their
own; all the pedants and doctrinaires whose queasy
stomachs retch at the thought of England's greatness,
who put scales on their eyes, and wax in their ears and
slime on their tongues to prove that England is always
in the wrong, all the greensick little aguecheeks who
exhibit the babyish workings of their deranged livers
as the holy motions of conscience, who will fight for
nothing but to keep out of a fight, and who would
rather that England should be struck to the heart than
that their shivering skins should be scratched—with all
the rest of the pitiable fry, engendered by luxury and a
long peace, who have made us a laughing-stock alike to
our enemies, to our dominions, to our allies, and to our-
selves. It was these mannikins and addleheads that
Germany sampled and mistook for Englishmen, and
then, promising herself an easy victory, gaily marched
out to war.

Surely Shakespeare, if he were alive to-day, would
sound his silver bugle and lead the chase that shall drive
them into their last burrow holes in the nethermost ob-
scurities of contempt and oblivion. For search him
through and through, and not a word shall you find that
can be twisted into approval of their lunes, while the
spirit that breathes throughout his work and inflames
some of his chiefest scenes, visits them in almost every
play with unmistakable messages of lofty rebuke and
scorn.

But again, it needs the super-subtle insight of German
criticism to detect in Shakespeare an enthusiastic sympathy with Germany, or the German nature, or the German policy and aims. If Shakespeare has any affection
for Germany, he has the strangest way of dissembling it.
It is true that mine host of the Garter says, "Germans
are honest men." But mine host is an incorrigible
blagueur. And he offers no proof that he was any judge
of Germans It is questionable whether he could have

stood cross-examination on the point And further, his experience of Germans does not extend over the last ten years However, let the Germans take what sorry morsel of comfort they can from mine host of the Garter He is the only one of Shakespeare's characters who has anything but abuse for Germans

There is an unkind reference to German women in the first act of "Henry V," where the Archbishop of Canterbury expounds the Salic law, which he says was established because certain Frenchmen held " in disdain the German women for some dishonest manners of their life" But it is obviously the Archbishop, and not Shakespeare, who is speaking.

Amongst the scanty references to Germans in Shakespeare there are only two that have any significance. One of these occurs in the " Merchant of Venice " and the other in " Cymbeline " But each of these fragments reveals Shakespeare's private feelings towards Germans in the most unmistakable way.

The well-known passage between Nerissa and Portia has already been noticed in the English papers.

Says Nerissa to Portia, " How like you the young German, the Duke of Saxony's nephew ? " " Very vilely in the morning when he is sober," Portia replies; "and most vilely in the afternoon when he is drunk. When he is best, he is little worse than a man, and when he is worst, he is little better than a beast."

That speech must be the expression of Shakespeare's own feelings For it has no apparent dramatic necessity or value. He could scarcely have written it if he had any affection or esteem for any living German He could scarcely have written it unless he had experienced some unpleasant contact with Germans, or unless their odious habits and natures were so well known that he could make a general unqualified reference to them before a popular audience At any rate there the speech stands, either as the expression of his private feelings, or of the popular experience and opinion of Germans

which he abundantly shared Without redress, without
qualification, Shakespeare frankly calls them drunken
beasts. It doesn't promise well for future peace and
comfort if Shakespeare is henceforth to make his spiritual
home in Germany.

But this passage was written in the prime of his early
manhood. Perhaps he changed his opinions in the years
that passed between the "Merchant of Venice" and
"Cymbeline" It is possible that in the meantime
Shakespeare may have visited Germany with his fellow
players, and thus have gained a better acquaintance
with the people whom he so cruelly vilified Let us in-
vite the German critics to turn to "Cymbeline." In the
fifth scene of the second act, Posthumus receives from
Iachimo the incontestable proofs of Imogen's infidelity
It is only the supreme poets that can give a tongue to
the great simple agonies and joys of life. In a speech
worthy to be wondered at with the same wonder that
holds us when we watch the like torrents of volcanic
jealousy as they flow from the lips of Othello—in a speech
worthy of Shakespeare and Othello at their height and
of none beside—in one of his most Shakespearean
speeches, Shakespeare lends utterance to the tortured
Posthumus. His jealousy gathers and rises in quick
gusts and bursts of revengeful fury, till midway in its
sweep, it plays round the maddening thought of Imogen's
actual surrender to Iachimo.

> O all the devils!
> This yellow Iachimo, in an hour—was 't not?—
> Or less,—at first?—perchance he spoke not, but
> Like a full acorned boar, a German one,—

We check, and question Shakespeare. Why "a *German*
one"? We then return to Posthumus and sweep on with
him in his whirlwind of implacable wrath and hate for
all womankind

We go back to Shakespeare and insist upon a reason
for this curious glancing interjection, "A *German* one."

Why not leave it at " Like a full acorned boar " ?
The image is complete there, ear and sense are ful-
filled. It is a coarse image, necessarily, intentionally,
and appropriately coarse, recalling the kindred appropriately coarse word pictures of Iago. The situation
requires a coarse, vivid, compact image. But when it is
once uttered dramatic propriety is satisfied Why then
this useless, digressionary " A *German* one " ?

Posthumus had come out to Rome by way of Milford
Haven and the sea. He could not have encountered any
German boars on his voyage. Iachimo, who is likened
to a German boar, is a Roman; or rather an Italian.
Italians may be happily different from Germans, but
Italian boars must be very much like German boars. It
would need a skilled naturalist to distinguish them. But
if there are any temperamental or morphological differ-
ences between Italian boars and German boars, surely
Iachimo would be more like an Italian boar than a
German one. Why then "a German one"? It is a poetic
fault, a dramatic lapse, and a physiological error

Why then does Shakespeare arrest Posthumus in the
very torrent, tempest, and whirlwind of his jealousy to
throw out a glancing jibe of his own, and implicitly to
call the Germans " lustful hogs"?

The phrase very clearly manifests Shakespeare's own
personal opinion of Germans, and his feelings towards
them For if he used it carefully and with consideration,
it shows that Shakespeare in the height and abandon-
ment of one of his tremendous speeches, was yet pre-
occupied with an intense dislike for Germans. And if
he used it unwittingly and without consideration, it
shows that his sub-conscious mind was stored with me-
mories of their unpleasant habits and qualities, and that
he had an instinctive repulsion for their persons.

And be it remembered that the Shakespeare who calls
the Germans lustful hogs, was the later Shakespeare, the
Shakespeare of increasing gentleness and humanity, of
ripened opinions, and matured wisdom, and enlarged

outlook. His feelings towards Germans had not changed
in the dozen or fifteen years that passed between " The
Merchant of Venice " and " Cymbeline ", unless German
criticism with its profound insight can interpret the
transition from "drunken beasts" to "lustful hogs" as
revealing Shakespeare's growing disposition to be com-
plimentary to them. Plain readers will rather interpret
it as a synthetic addition to his earlier summary estimate
of the German nature

And this is the poet whom Germans claim as their
own, and delight to honour with a tercentenary celebration—the poet who ignores them except on two marked
occasions, when he stops and turns aside from his
dramatic beat to abuse and insult them! Surely when
they have examined him a little more closely they will
give second thoughts a chance and cancel their Shakespeare anniversary festival. Why should they honour
and fête him when he discovers such a cordial antipathy
to his hosts, and is so evidently determined to make
things unpleasant at his own birthday party? It shows
a new and unsuspected vein of rare generosity in the
German character, thus to honour and kindly treat their
enemy Why should they do it? Except that after the
war they may be able to boast that they treated with
magnanimity at least one hapless Englishman who fell
into their hands But can the Germans suppose that if
Shakespeare were alive to-day, he would use them except for his wash-pot, and to cast over them the shoe of
his angry derision?

Far otherwise, and in what a different temper does
Shakespeare treat the French and France He had little
to do with Germany, apparently he had an instinctive
aversion from Germans He has but a poor score of references to them and their country, two of them, as we
have seen, reveal an intense dislike that must needs break
out in abuse All the rest are merely casual and in-
different

But he had much to do with France and Frenchmen,

especially in his historical plays. And from this we have a curious result Shakespeare's references to France are far more numerous than his references to England, to the French far more numerous than to the English, while he mentions "Frenchman" twice as often as he mentions "Englishman."

Though as English dramatist and historian he had at times to give the French a hard, official rap and a contemptuous word, yet it would be difficult to find any sign of personal malice or even dislike. Talbot, in the first part of "Henry VI," speaks of a little herd of "England's timorous deer" being "mazed with a yelping kennel of French curs." But this is Talbot speaking in perfect dramatic propriety as an English soldier. It is not polite, but it is mild compared with "drunken beasts" and "lustful hogs" Shakespeare, in his allusions to France, nowhere intrudes with an insulting epithet of his own

His general bearing towards France, so far as it departs from the strict impartiality of the dramatist, is one rather of genial respect and liking, as towards a worthy foe, who has to be honourably thrashed, or from whom an honourable thrashing has to be received; always with a view to an honourable peace, and a hope of future friendship The most fatal mistake Germany has made in this war, has been to wage it so as to leave her enemies no loophole for future friendship with her; no present hope or desire or aim but to put her into perpetual outlawry from the brotherhood of nations

The most winsome scene of courtship between Henry the Fifth and Katherine may not unfairly be taken as a clue to Shakespeare's feelings and attitude towards France It is alive and pulsing with goodwill, and with hearty good humour. Not even a German professor can picture Shakespeare writing a kindred scene with a German Katherine. That task would have been too heavy even for Shakespeare's imagination, had it not first been too repugnant to his feelings. Germans will doubtless be interested in another passage in that last scene of " Henry V "—the benediction which Shakespeare, through the lips of the French queen, pronounces upon the marriage of France and England—one of his happiest prophecies The timely moment of its fulfilment is surely the timeliest moment for Germans to con it over and get it by heart

> God, the best maker of all marriages,
> Combine your hearts in one, your realms in one!
> So be there 'twixt your kingdoms such a spousal
> That never may ill office, or fell jealousy,
> Thrust in between the pactions of these kingdoms,
> To make divorce of their incorporate league,
> That English may as French, French Englishmen,
> Receive each other. God speak this Amen!

Here again, Shakespeare with his unerring prevision seems to be sending Germans his birthday message for 1916, assuring them that France and England are indissolubly united, and that no device will serve to part them, and bring about a separate peace. So full is Shakespeare of apt admonitions and lucky instances and illustrations, if Germans will but read him aright.

How absurd and groundless are German claims upon Shakespeare, may be seen when they are compared with the claims that France might put forth if she chose If in this tercentenary year France chose to acclaim Shakespeare for her own poet, she could advance a case out of all measure stronger than the German claim. For Shakespeare himself, instead of flouting her as he flouts the Germans, could be brought to support her and to testify to his love and admiration for her

He throws her many an amiable glance. Twice he calls her " this best garden of the world," " our fertile France "; he speaks of " her lovely visage "——How would he speak of France to-day! How would his heart burn and his tongue catch fire now, when every hour brings the breathless tidings of Verdun! O France, faithful ally, inspiring comrade, fast-locked friend, best loved of all lands by all men, save their own land, first in all the graces and civilities of common everyday life; first in all the arts of peace, and first in all the chivalries of war; first in the delicacies of sense, and first in the delicacies of the spirit, first in clear, sane thought, and bright, jewelled word, and kindling heroic deed, lonely mistress of Shakespeare's own art—how shall any English tongue, ay, even Shakespeare's, tell of thy wonderful deeds, of thy prodigal sacrifices, thy iron fortitude, thy massive patience, thy inexorable resolve, thy valour beyond all mortal pitch and compass?

If Shakespeare lived to-day, how willingly would we lend him to thee—nay, share him with thee—to sing with thy own poets of thy victories and ours; from the far-spread scurrying Marne to stubborn, hardset, indomitable Verdun; and onwards to the gathering clash of great fierce battles to come; through supernal fervours and agonies to the sure final triumph, to the last great day of account when the righteous forfeit shall be called, and enforced to the uttermost farthing!

How would Shakespeare swell his proudest notes to praise thee, and yet not praise thee enough! And turning from this havoc and ruin, how would he send his prophetic soul to dream of things to come, of the days when these bloodstains shall be washed from the face of Europe, and the earth shall be green again; when thy land shall be cleansed from abominable hoofs, and thy cities shall be redeemed and redressed in new arising loveliness, and thou, forgetting these long past harvests of blood and death, shalt dwell securely amongst thy sunny plains and vineyards, with customary harvests of corn and wine, handfast with roused, revitalized England, jocund and fecund with countless increase of innumerable sons, filling all the void places of their inalienable heritage to its utmost borders!

O France, endure! England shall not fail thee! Many of our dearest, bravest dead are with thee, sacred morsels of thy soil, dust of thy dust, irrevocably thine, incorporate citizens of France, whose crumbling hands wave to us from the clods to uphold thee to the end, whose silenced lips do ceaselessly reiterate our lasting covenant with thee that England shall not fail thee   O France, endure, endure!

But again, what likeness, what spiritual affinity do Germans find between themselves and Shakespeare that they should wish to seduce him from England?

The Germans are a warlike nation, loving war for its own sake, glorifying it, and lately glorifying cruelty and bloodshed and murder. There runs through Shakespeare an evident admiration for the pomp and circumstance of war, for its glittering momentum; its drums and pride   More evident still is his love for soldiers and soldiership   It is another of his dominant prepossessions.

For war itself, its cruelties and miseries and disorders, he seems to have nothing but hatred. And he has a lively sense of the material value and advantages of peace   But he apprehends that a long peace is the dangerous breeder of sloth and vice, and fatty decay   He would make a turbulent guest at a tea-party of our peace-politicians. Let them not waste their time in reading him   Let them expel him from their bookshelves. Facts, the plainest and sternest do not convince them; neither will Shakespeare, neither would they be persuaded though one rose from the dead

In the matters of peace and war, as in all the great issues of life, Shakespeare holds an even, balanced mind   He seems to accept war as an inevitable recurrence, a frightful, glorious evil, with some soul of goodness

He has a favourite type of soldier, in whom is manifest the English character at its best   All Shakespeare's characters are Englishmen. His Romans, Greeks, and Italians are English —English in the marrow that nourishes their bones, and in the blood that warms their veins—Englishmen first, and Romans, Greeks, and Italians afterwards   But his Englishmen are ten times

Englishmen; as was Shakespeare himself. In this type
of soldier—Falconbridge, Hotspur, Henry V, Mercutio—
Shakespeare must have drawn largely upon himself
We hear his own voice speaking so often through them
If anyone wishes to know what Shakespeare was like
from thirty to thirty-five, he may get some idea from
studying these soldiers, with others that show occa-
sional similar traits. A composite Falconbridge-Hot-
spur-Henry-Mercutio would give a not unfair early
portrait of Shakespeare. It would indeed be partial and
inadequate, but it would not be deceptive Shakespeare was much more than they; but everyone of them
is Shakespeare's own brother or cousin

High chivalry, punctilious honour, spontaneous magnanimity, careless generosity, and a rich abounding
humour native in the English midlands—these are the
birthmarks they derive from Shakespeare What kin-
ship, what obscure sign of a hundredth degree of cousin-
hood, do Germans find between these soldier gentlemen
of Shakespeare and their own machine-driven levies,
their pirates and gas-poisoners, with all their other pro-
geny of Tarquin, and Herod, and Barabbas?

One soldier, indeed, Shakespeare has drawn in whom
Germans may behold the true and dreadful image of
themselves—Macbeth

"Macbeth," we learn, is the play chosen to be the
German national offering to Shakespeare It is to be
performed on 23rd April with great solemnity at the
Court Theatre, Weimar

And thou so near, Goethe! Thou, who more than any
other, made known thy great elder brother to thy people!
If England has strayed far from Shakespeare, and has
rooted herself at ease on Lethe's wharf, scarcely com-
prehending the voice of her greatest golden-mouth'd
son, stupidly travelling her round, and letting die out
of her life, glory and genius and joy—if England has
departed from Shakespeare, how much farther has
Germany departed from thee, Goethe? How aloof and

remote art thou, great dead oracle, from this welter of
strife, and these abysms of blood and terror wherein thy
countrymen are plunged! With what calm, majestic
reproof dost thou hold thyself apart from these Germans,
as alien from thee as they are alien from Shakespeare.
They have claimed Shakespeare from us We will not
claim thee, Goethe, from them, for Germany has much
more need of thee We will leave thee to minister to
her when she wakes from her insane fever dreams

And they will play " Macbeth " within a short hail
of thee Heed them not, Goethe, nor intrude at their
festival to reveal to them that they are making a
dreadful mimicry of the tragedy of their own fate No
warning or admonition from thee can arrest them now
Heed them not, Goethe, but slumber on!

What evil angel of their destiny tempted the Germans
to choose Macbeth for their anniversary offering to
Shakespeare, in this year of all others? It is the very
picture of their own character marching to its ruin.
Therein Shakespeare, with predeterminate insight and
precise emphasis limns their exactest likeness; con-
ducts them step by step through each successive act
and circumstance to their appointed end Never has
history or fiction so faithfully engraved so truthful a
parallel.

When the curtain shall rise at Weimar on 23rd April,
and for ever after when the curtain shall rise on " Macbeth " in any German theatre, let each member of the
audience watch how cunningly Shakespeare has enfolded
the story of Germany within the story of " Macbeth "
Let German playgoers glance back at the great and
valorous soldier, full of dauntless courage, and unsuspected loyalty, a brave man, " full of the milk of human
kindness "—such a Germany do we seem to remember—
" what he would highly, that he would holily "—" was
not without ambition "—that is, at the first he had but a
very moderate ambition This was Macbeth.

But he eats of the insane root, and instantly all the

unknown powers of evil without him solicit and inspire
to action the unknown powers of evil within him. From
the first moment that the witches call to him, his de-
struction is sealed Swiftly the lust of power infects
all his veins, the impulses of his insatiable ambition become the law of his universe, he screams and raves for
sovereign sway and masterdom, with treachery, cruelty,
and blind malice, he strikes down all that stands in his
way Crime, useless, purposeless crime, becomes his
hourly trade and delight, and all his thoughts pursue
bloodshed continually. Behold him, Germans, ravaging
and desolating Scotland as you have ravaged and desolated Belgium

> Each new morn
> New widows howl, new orphans cry, new sorrows
> Strike heaven on the face that it resounds
> As if it felt with Scotland, and yell'd out
> Like syllable of dolour

And again.

> Alas, poor country !
> Almost afraid to know itself It cannot
> Be called our mother, but our grave, where nothing
> But who knows nothing, is once seen to smite,
> Where sighs and groans and shrieks that rend the air
> Are made, not marked, where violent sorrow seems
> A modern ecstasy The dead man's knell
> Is there scarce asked for who, and good men's lives
> Expire before the flowers in their caps,
> Dying or ere they sicken

Why, even this is feeble when matched against the
realities of your wanton bloody tyrannies and crimes in
Belgium Even Shakespeare cannot render to you a
sufficient account of yourselves Yet when you shall hear
these words spoken on the Weimar stage, take them for
Shakespeare's living direct message to the German
nation, take them for his picture of yourselves and your
deeds, for Scotland is Belgium, and Macbeth is Germany

Oh well have you chosen Macbeth, German playgoers!
For follow him through, watch the impetus of past
crimes carrying him helplessly to greater crimes; see
him treacherously putting spies in all his neighbours'
houses; and here, in the very heyday and meridian of
widespread slaughter, he yet turns his first thoughts to
contrive the murder of a helpless woman and her children! Is it to see a bloody tyrant murdering defenceless
women and children that you play "Macbeth," O German
lovers of Shakespeare? For very shame avoid that scene
—unless indeed your hands are so subdued to what they
work in, that they will applaud the murderer of Mac-
duff's child on the stage at Weimar, as your whole
nation to-day applauds your own child murderers. But
follow the play.

Macbeth begins to distrust the flattering auguries that
have beckoned him to his ruin Were they not also
lying prophets that prophesied victory to you? As the
witches to Macbeth, as Zedekiah to Ahab, so have they
lied in whom you trusted Behold in the witches your
own false prophets. Do you begin to read the message
of "Macbeth" to Germany to-day? Ah! watch it closely
as Claudius watched the play, and with like feelings,
for surely it is your own story Marry this is miching
mallecho. It means mischief

Go with Macbeth to the pit of Acheron. That appari-
tion of Banquo and his long succession of inheritors—
can you not interpret it, German playgoers? Macbeth
has sought to cut off Banquo and his posterity, even as
you sought to cut off England. Read the parable. When
Banquo appears at the pit of Acheron on that Weimar
stage, see England take his place, and, smiling, point to
the long line of her inheriting children, carrying the
sceptres of dominion to future ages—Canada, Australia,
New Zealand, Africa, Egypt, India—see the line stretches
out to the crack of doom And England smiles upon
thee, Germany, and points at them for hers. Look into
that glass of the future, and read the parable Remem-

ber Germany's design to destroy England, see how it has recoiled as Macbeth's murder of Banquo recoiled Its great effect has been to bring all England's children round her to defend her, and to make her vast Empire one family, secure and complete With that remembrance, how will these words fall upon your ears, German playgoers? Hear Germany speaking in her character of Macbeth.

> If this be so
> For England's issue have I filed my mind,
> Put rancours in the vessel of my peace
> Only for them, and mine eternal jewel
> Given to the common enemy of man,
> To make them Kings, the seed of England Kings

On to the last scenes—England has gathered her forces against the tyrant Nay, sit it out—stay till all the gigantic tragedy is done—breathlessly follow the tyrant from the pit of Acheron or Verdun to his inevitable doom Watch him leaping from desperate savagery to desperate savagery; he fights and fights with matchless bravery and courage, all his authentic auguries betray him, yet he fights on, fights, fights, till he falls hacked and dismembered, like a furious beast And the earth is clean of him.

Oh well have you chosen " Macbeth " for your festival play, German playgoers! Well and faithfully will Shakespeare serve you! Ponder him deeply, now that at last the slow, immitigable might of England has begun to encompass you

CHISWICK PRESS PRINTED BY CHARLES WHITTINGHAM AND CO
TOOKS COURT, CHANCERY LANE, LONDON

Lightning Source UK Ltd.
Milton Keynes UK
UKOW02f2140171213

223220UK00006B/45/P